SPACE MISSIONS™

The *Endeavour* Mission STS-61

Fixing the Hubble Space Telescope

Helen Zelon

The Rosen Publishing Group's
PowerKids Press™
New York

For Anna "LW" Sasson, tender, inquisitive, and sure of her own mind

Published in 2002 by The Rosen Publishing Group, Inc.
29 East 21st Street, New York, NY 10010

First Edition

Book Design: Michael de Guzman
Project Editors: Jennifer Landau, Jason Moring, Jennifer Quasha

Photo credits: pp. 4, 7, 8, 11, 15, 19, 20 © Photri-Microstock; p. 12 © NASA/Roger Ressmeyer/CORBIS; p.16 © Hulton Getty/Archive Photos.

Zelon, Helen.
The Endeavour mission STS-61 : fixing the Hubble Space Telescope /Helen Zelon.
    p. cm. — (Space missions)
Includes bibliographical references and index.
ISBN 0-8239-5774-8 (library binding)
1. Endeavour (Space shuttle)—Juvenile literature. 2. Space flights—Juvenile literature. 3. Extravehicular activity
(Manned space flight)—Juvenile literature. 4. Hubble Space Telescope (Spacecraft)—Juvenile literature. [1. Endeavour (Space shuttle)
2. Manned space flight. 3. Extravehicular activity (Manned space flight) 4. Hubble Space Telescope (Spacecraft).—Maintenance and repair.]
I.Title. II. Series.
TL795.515 .Z45 2002
629.44'1—dc21
                                                                    00-013089

Manufactured in the United States of America

Contents

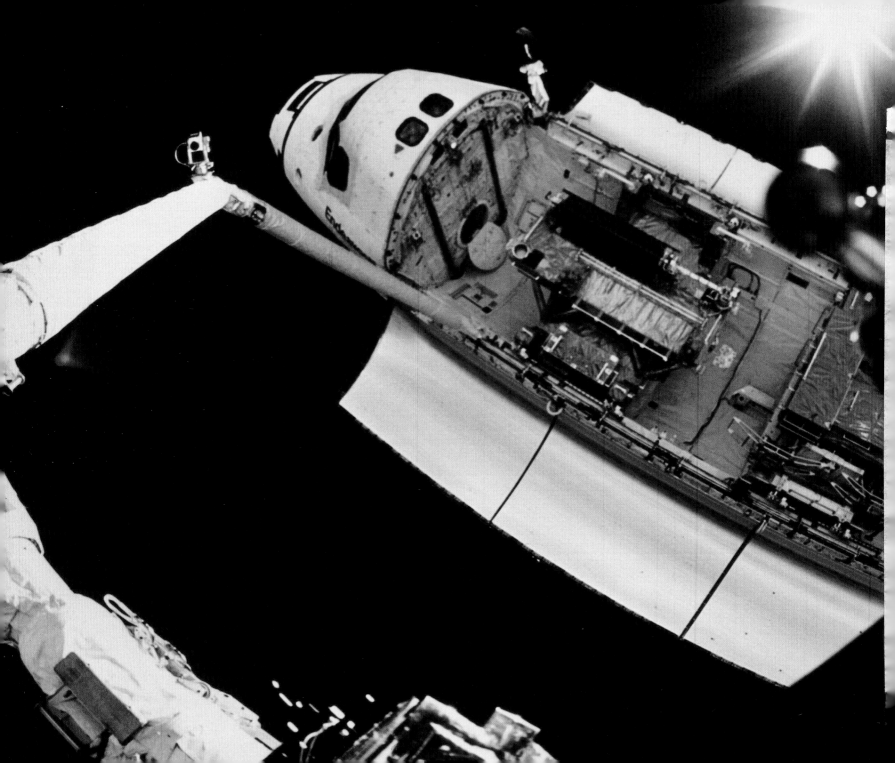

Shuttle Bus in the Sky

In the 1980s, scientists and engineers at **NASA developed** a new kind of spacecraft, called the space shuttle. The space shuttle goes to space, returns to Earth, and goes into space again. Each time it takes new passengers and new **cargo**. The space shuttle can be used to place **satellites** into **orbit**. It can move people and supplies to and from a future space station. Shuttle astronauts can conduct scientific and medical tests in orbit. The trunk of the space shuttle is called the **payload bay**. Astronauts can open the doors of the payload bay to release cargo into space. When its mission is complete, the space shuttle returns to Earth. It lands on the ground like an airplane. The space shuttle can be used over and over to do important work in space.

← *This picture shows the inside of the* Endeavour *and its cargo bay, which holds goods needed for a spaceflight.*

Hubble in Trouble

The Hubble Space Telescope was released into space on April 24, 1990, by the space shuttle *Discovery*. Sending a telescope into space would help **astronomers** see and understand more about space than they ever could from Earth. The Hubble had equipment to send the pictures it took back to Earth. The Hubble telescope **launch** went smoothly, but the telescope began having problems once it was in space. The Hubble's mirrors had something wrong with them. The size of one large mirror was off by a tiny bit, far less than the width of one human hair. The mirror problems made the pictures that the Hubble sent back to Earth fuzzy and unclear. Other parts of the telescope were not working well, either. Something had to be done to fix the Hubble.

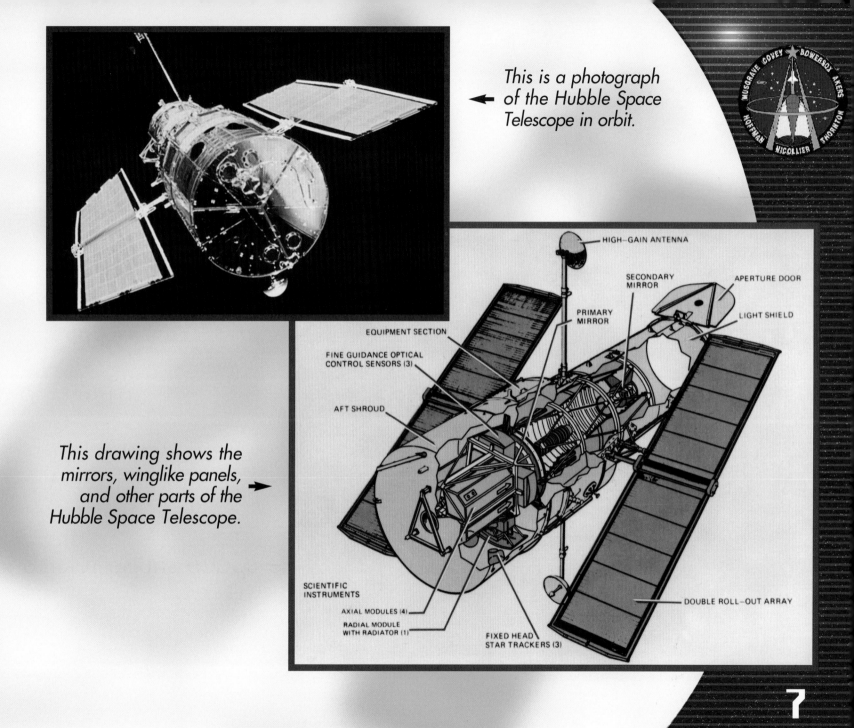

This is a photograph of the Hubble Space Telescope in orbit.

This drawing shows the mirrors, winglike panels, and other parts of the Hubble Space Telescope.

HIGH—GAIN ANTENNA

SECONDARY MIRROR

APERTURE DOOR

PRIMARY MIRROR

LIGHT SHIELD

EQUIPMENT SECTION

FINE GUIDANCE OPTICAL CONTROL SENSORS (3)

AFT SHROUD

DOUBLE ROLL—OUT ARRAY

SCIENTIFIC INSTRUMENTS

AXIAL MODULES (4)

RADIAL MODULE WITH RADIATOR (1)

FIXED HEAD STAR TRACKERS (3)

Practice Makes Perfect

Kenneth Bowersox and Richard Covey were *Endeavour's* pilot and mission commander. Claude Nicollier worked the shuttle's robot arm, which helped the astronauts make repairs outside the space shuttle. Story Musgrave, M.D., Jeffrey Hoffman, Kathryn Thornton, and Thomas Akers were the astronauts who made up two teams of "space **mechanics**."

On Earth, **gravity** gives people and objects weight. In space there is no gravity. To prepare for being weightless in space, the astronauts trained in a 35-foot-deep (10.7-m-deep) swimming pool. The *Endeavour* crew practiced on an underwater model of the Hubble. The astronauts also learned to "ride" the shuttle's robot arm. They were attached to the robot arm by their boots. With their feet secured, the astronauts had both hands free to make repairs.

← *This is a photograph of Claude Nicollier, who worked the Endeavour's robot arm.*

Ready, Set, Liftoff

Before dawn on December 1, 1993, the *Endeavour* crew got into their space suits. They got on the shuttle at Kennedy Space Center in Florida. As the sun rose, clouds moved in. Strong winds began to blow. During a launch, strong rockets carry the spacecraft into orbit. NASA engineers and scientists worried about what would happen if something went wrong and the shuttle had to make an **emergency** landing. Too much wind could prevent a safe landing. The launch would have to wait another day.

December 2 dawned bright and clear. The winds were calm. The crew got on the shuttle again. At 4:27 A.M., the 4,511,115-pound (2,046,207-kg) shuttle rode into space.

This is a photograph of the Endeavour *at the Kennedy Space Center in Florida.* ➤

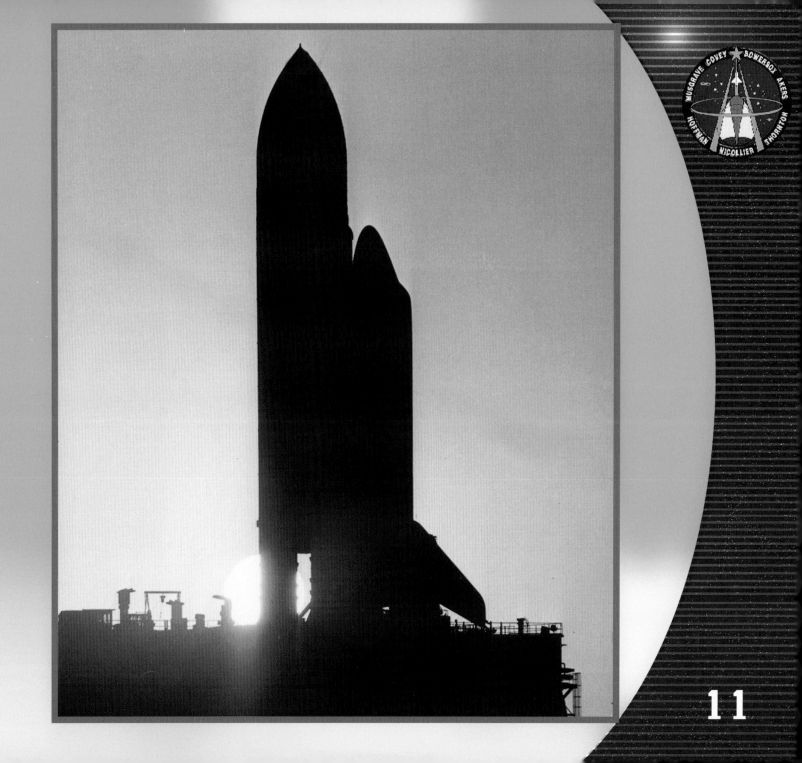

Life in Space

Shortly after launch, the crew changed out of their space suits and into comfortable clothes. The clothes had to be washed and dried many times before the mission. This was to make sure that bits of lint didn't float into the space shuttle's equipment and damage it. Early astronauts ate food from tubes that looked like toothpaste tubes. The *Endeavour* crew's food was packaged like TV dinners. There is no gravity in space, so food that falls from a fork floats around the crew **compartment**. If some juice "spilled," it formed a ball and floated in the air. The astronauts had to catch the ball of juice with a straw. To sleep, the crew used sleeping bags that attached with Velcro to the walls and ceiling of the space shuttle.

This is a picture of the Endeavour *crew during the STS-61 mission. In the top row (from left to right) are astronauts Story Musgrave, Jeffrey Hoffman, Kathryn Thornton, and Thomas Akers. In the bottom row (from left to right) are astronauts Claude Nicollier, Kenneth Bowersox, and Richard Covey.*

13

Capturing the Hubble

Just after midnight on December 5, 1993, the *Endeavour* crew was close to the Hubble Space Telescope. The telescope was 43 feet (13 m) long, with large, winglike panels, called arrays, on two sides. It would not be easy to move. The shuttle crew had to capture the Hubble and bring it into the shuttle's payload bay to begin repairs. Astronauts Bowersox and Covey used bursts of power from the shuttle's rockets to move closer to the Hubble. The astronauts only had enough fuel for one try to catch the telescope. The shuttle glided under the Hubble. The payload bay doors opened to make room for the telescope. Then astronaut Claude Nicollier reached out and captured the broken Hubble with the robot arm. He moved the telescope into the payload bay for repairs.

This is a picture of the Hubble Space Telescope inside the Endeavour's payload bay. ➤

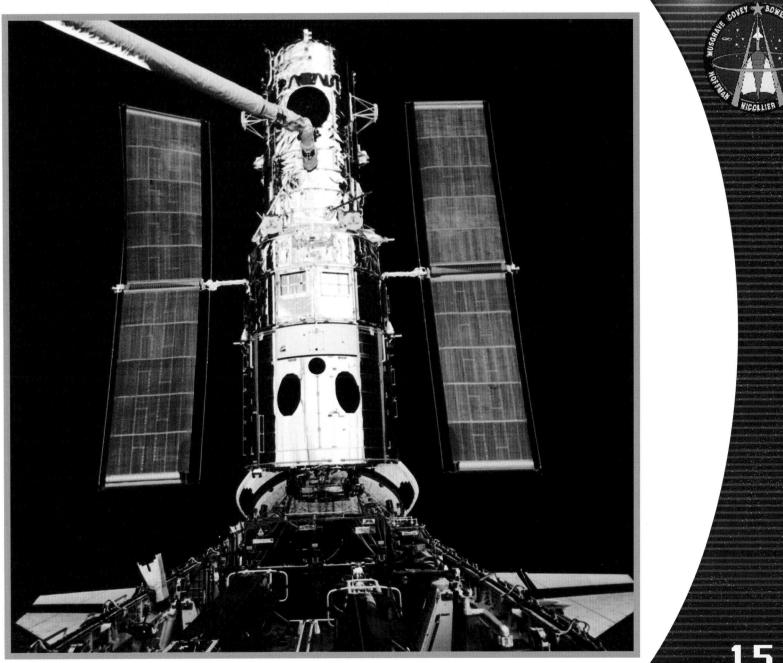

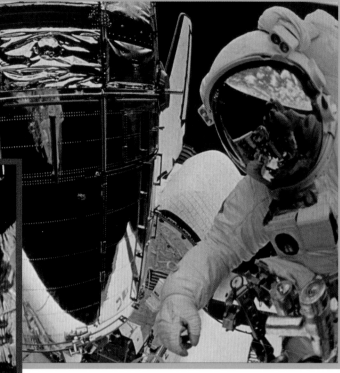

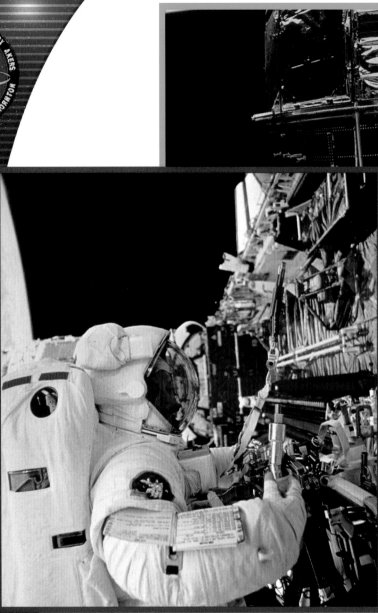

This is a picture of astronaut Story Musgrave during one of three space walks he took on mission STS-61.

This photograph shows astronaut Kathy Thornton working to repair the Hubble Space Telescope.

Space Mechanics

To fix the Hubble, the astronauts had to leave the shuttle and "walk" in space. During **space walks**, astronauts are attached to the shuttle by a long cord. A space suit protects an astronaut from the extreme heat and cold of space. It also holds a supply of air for the astronaut to breathe. Space walks can take 8 hours or more, and astronauts can get hungry and thirsty. Space suits have built-in snack pouches. One pouch holds a drink with a straw, and the other has a fruit snack or granola bar for quick energy. The *Endeavour* crew worked in two-person teams to fix the Hubble's **gyroscopes** and mirrors. They installed new equipment to give the Hubble more power to see into the galaxy. The astronauts were proud of the work they had done.

Night Walking

Astronauts Thornton and Akers had to replace the damaged solar arrays. The arrays were made to roll up like window shades. Kathy Thornton rolled up one array. Tom Akers put it in the payload bay. The second array was broken and had to be thrown over the side of the shuttle and off into space. The array held an electrical charge when it was warmed by the Sun. If the astronauts touched the array in sunlight, the charge could hurt them. This meant they had to remove the array in darkness. They separated the broken array from the Hubble. Riding the robot arm, Kathy Thornton held the broken array overhead. Claude Nicollier turned the robot arm away from the Hubble. Thornton let go of the array. The panel floated through the sky like a big, silver wing.

This picture shows Kathy Thornton (right) working to repair the Hubble Space Telescope. She is connected to the Endeavour's robot arm by her feet. On the left is astronaut Tom Akers.

The Great Screw Chase

On the third space walk, Story Musgrave and Jeff Hoffman saw a tiny screw floating nearby. It had gotten loose and was bobbing along close to the Hubble telescope. If it fell into the telescope, the Hubble could be badly broken. Hoffman was riding the robot arm. Claude Nicollier was at the controls. Hoffman's thick gloves made it hard to grab the little screw, but he finally caught it. The Hubble had been held in place in the payload bay while the astronauts made their repairs. It was time to release the Hubble into the sky. With a burst of the shuttle's engine, the spacecraft pulled away, leaving the Hubble floating where the payload bay had been. The Hubble was on its own and in orbit again.

← *This is a photograph of astronaut Jeff Hoffman on the robot arm of the* Endeavour.

Bound for Earth Again

As the *Endeavour* headed back to Earth, the astronauts celebrated their hard work. Jeff Hoffman had brought a **Hanukkah menorah** and a **dreidel** on board, and the astronauts had a Hanukkah party in space. Without gravity, the dreidel never stopped spinning and never fell down! After spending 11 days in space and traveling 4.4 million miles (7.1 million km), it was time to come home. On December 13, 1993, the *Endeavour* glided smoothly down at Cape Canaveral in Florida. A month later, pictures from the repaired Hubble were made public. The repairs were a success! Today the Hubble is still sending images to Earth. We continue to learn about the galaxy that surrounds us thanks to the "space mechanics" of the *Endeavour*.

Glossary

astronomers (uh-STRAH-nuh-merz) People who study the Sun, Moon, planets, and stars.

cargo (KAR-goh) Goods or merchandise carried by a vehicle, such as an airplane, ship, train, or space shuttle.

compartment (kum-PART-ment) A separate section of something.

developed (dih-VEH-lupt) To have worked out in great detail.

dreidel (DRAY-del) A four-sided top.

emergency (ih-MUR-jin-see) An event that happens when quick help is needed.

gravity (GRA-vih-tee) The natural force that causes objects to move or tend to move toward the center of Earth.

gyroscopes (JY-ruh-skohps) Toplike objects used to keep balance and direction.

Hanukkah (HAH-nuh-kah) A Jewish winter holiday commemorating the rededication of the Temple in Jerusalem.

launch (LAWNCH) When a spacecraft is pushed out or put into the air.

mechanics (mih-KA-niks) People who are skilled at fixing machines.

menorah (meh-NOR-uh) A nine-branched candleholder, lit every night during Hanukkah.

NASA (NA-suh) National Aeronautics and Space Administration, the United States's space agency.

orbit (OR-bit) The path one body makes around another, usually larger, body.

payload bay (PAY-load BAY) The "trunk" of a space shuttle, where the payload is stored.

satellites (SA-til-eyets) Human-made or natural objects that orbit another body.

space walks (SPAYS WOKS) Movement by an astronaut outside of a space capsule.

Index

Web Sites

To find out more about the *Endeavour* Mission STS-61 and spaceflight, check out these Web sites:

http://spaceflight.nasa.gov

www.jsc.nasa.gov